Ultimate Topiaries

The Most Magnificent Horticultural Art Through the Years

Elizabeth Buckley

AN IMPRINT OF RUNNING PRESS
PHILADELPHIA • LONDON

This edition published in the United States in 2004 by
Courage Books, an imprint of Running Press Book Publishers
125 South Twenty-second Street,
Philadelphia,PA 19103-4399

9 8 7 6 5 4 3 2 1

Digit on the right indicates the number of this printing

Library of Congress Number[2003116005]

ISBN 0-7624-1942-3

Notice: The information contained in this book is true and complete to
the best of our knowledge. All recommendations are made without any
guarantee on the part of the author or publisher. The author and publisher
disclaim all liability in connection with the use of this information.

Designer: Philip Clucas MSIAD
Printed and bound in Taiwan

This book may be ordered by mail from the publisher.
But try your bookstore first!
Visit us on the web at *www.runningpress.com*

Contents

The History of Topiary

'Even the clipt yews interest me, and if I found one in any garden that should be mine, in the shape of a peacock, I should be as proud to keep his tail well spread as the man who first carved him.' *ROBERT SOUTHEY (1774-1843)*

According to the American Boxwood Society (which was founded in 1961 by a group of professional and amateur enthusiasts) boxwood (*buxus sempervirens*) - probably the most versatile and popular of topiary plants - is the oldest garden ornamental known to man. So it is hardly surprising that the ancient Egyptians were using box for topiary over 6000 years ago, clipped into ornamental hedges. Tradition has it that the first inspiration for topiary was plants grazed into bizarre shapes by browsing animals. Even today, we can see wild plants moulded into curious forms by a combination of natural phenomena, such as the prevailing wind and animal nibbling. Box is fabulously versatile, being not only a landscape plant, but a source of lumber that even has medicinal properties. According to the ABS, leaf and fruit fossils from boxwood have been located in more than 20 separate locations throughout Europe, dating back as far as twenty-two million years...

Left: *This classically inspired parterre is designed around a topiary pineapple, the traditional sign of welcome.*

Although topiary was known and practiced in Ancient Greece, it would appear that the Western tradition of topiary came down to us via the gardeners of Ancient Rome. The very word itself comes from the Latin for ornamental gardening, 'topiarius'. The Romans looked to the East for inspiration in their gardens, as in so many other facets of life, and adopted the Egyptian use of clipped forms and statuary. Pliny the Elder ascribes the introduction of topiary to Rome to Gnaius Mattius (38 BC to 14 AD), and it is likely that Mattius used the topiaries of these earlier civilizations as his inspiration. Pliny the Younger describes his Tuscan gardens as being embellished with topiary sculptures of animals, figures and obelisks, together with clipped hedges in box and other evergreens.

Above: *This herb-filled parterre echoes those originally grown in monastery gardens for medicinal use.*

The use of both topiary and statuary are as fresh and popular today as they were then, moving with the times, and providing a classical reference to the gardens of the past at one and the same time. To this day, topiary is especially popular in Italy, and some of the most extraordinary and complicated shapes are grown by commercial nurseries. Full-scale horse-drawn carriages, Mercedes Benz cars, massive dinosaurs – are all for sale at a high price. The dark green shapes of the more classical topiaries seem to blend naturally into the Italian landscape of formal planting and rows of finger cypresses.

Boxwood is the oldest garden ornamental known to man

But with the collapse of the Roman Empire (around 400 A.D.), the trappings of civilization were swept aside, and there was a return to the Dark Ages. Luxuries like gardening for pleasure were completely forgotten until the Renaissance period, preserved only in small oases such as monastery gardens and within castle walls. We only know about the

Left: *This stately group of long-established topiaries at Levens Hall is only a fragment of this world-class garden.*

Below: *These simple boxwood millstones make this cottage garden unique, the dark green shapes contrast with the white-painted brick.*

continued use of topiary during this time
through contemporary illuminated manuscripts.

With the onset of the Renaissance in the
fourteenth century (beginning in Italy, and
gradually spreading across Europe), a return to
affluence, and a fascination with all art forms,
ensured a resurgence of interest in topiary.
The artists and gardeners of the period looked
to classical times for their inspiration. Some of
their creations, such as the gardens at the Villa
Garzoni in Tuscany, still exist today. Leone
Alberti's design for the gardens of a Florence
villa (of 1459) included many topiary forms
'spheres, porticoes, temples, vases, urns, apes,
donkeys, oxen, a bear, giants, men and women,
warriors, a witch, philosophers, popes and
cardinals.'

The new interest in topiary proceeded to
France, always in the forefront of style
and elegance, and became a popular element
in gardens of fashion. 'Parterres' (hedges 'at
ground level') originated here. These are
complex patterns of low-growing plants.
Parterres seemed to appeal to the French love
of sophisticated ornament with a certain degree

of artifice. Taller clipped hedges were also used to frame vistas and obscure problem views in a way that persists today. The structure and immaculate precision of these topiary gardens seemed to suggest the power of man over nature, and Louis XIV's gardener, there was a huge upsurge in the use of topiary and clipping, particularly in the cultivation of fashionable mazes and labyrinths. These can be seen to this day at the palaces of the period, such as Hampton Court. This maze has just undergone a huge restoration. The tradition

In the whimsical spirit of Tudor times one poet described how 'Rosemary (is) cut out with curious order, in satyrs, centaurs, whales and half-men-horses.'

Le Notre, used miles of clipped hedging at Versailles to suggest the King's dominion, even over the natural order. The gardens were reputed to have cost over two billion francs in a display of astronomical extravagance.

In England, the tradition had survived the Dark Ages in monastery physic gardens. Monastic parterres were grown to provide a well-ordered supply of herbs for ministering to the sick. One such is recreated here in this low-hedged design of box filled with an abundance of herb varieties. This particular parterre was created for the Chelsea Flower Show in London, England in 1991. With the gradual spread of the Renaissance to England

also developed in the beautiful Tudor knot garden where colored gravel, or ornamental flowers in contrasting colors, were separated by the low-growing hedges. Knot gardens exist today in gardens such as the Tudor House Garden in Southampton, Hampshire. They have also developed into more modern forms, where plants of a far later introduction are included, such as this ultimately dramatic canna-filled knot garden of yellow alternanthea. This was created at Bill Smith and Dennis Schrader's Garden on Long Island and is a fantastic example of traditional forms brought bang up-to-date.

Ornamental and bizarre topiary was also very popular in the whimsical spirit of Tudor

Below: *This modern take on the parterre, at the Smith-Schrader garden on Long Island, is planted with canna petoria and yellow alternanthea.*

times. One poet described how 'Rosemary (is) cut out with curious order, in satyrs, centaurs, whales and half-men-horses.' This fantastical element very much embodies the idea of a garden being a paradise away from the insecurities and harsh realities of life especially in these politically turbulent and dangerous years.

In Holland, society was ordered along rather different lines, money being concentrated in the hands of the merchant and middle classes rather than the aristocracy or political elite. One-upmanship and conspicuous consumption were very much the order of the day. When you had an elegant town house filled with Old Masters, where next to turn one's attention but the garden? These were often quite small – much Dutch land had been reclaimed from the sea, and was consequently scarce and expensive. Topiary shapes were an ideal way of dramatically decorating these small formal schemes. Dutch enthusiasm went far beyond the usual classic shapes, and their gardens were often extravaganzas of sculptures of people, animals, birds and abstract forms – all in topiary. To this day, there is a huge market for topiary plants and equipment in Holland, and many are exported to the UK and other European markets.

When the Dutch King, William of Orange, inherited the British throne in 1688, he re-imported a fascination for this garden tradition to England, and topiary became a craze appealing to all levels of society. This became known as the 'Golden Age of Topiary'. During this period several gardens were created that still survive, including the world famous garden at Levens Hall in

Right: *Architectural cedar pillars offset the entrance to the vernacular oak-framed house at Stoneacre.*

Above: *This group of show topiaries represents many of the simpler shapes available commercially.*

Cumbria. More topiary varieties also came into play at this time, including yew and holly.

But with the advent of the Romantic Movement in the eighteenth century, when the untamed natural wilderness was celebrated by poets and writers, there was an inevitable backlash against the 'artificiality' of topiary. Joseph Addison wrote an article in 1712 in the Spectator magazine advocating the beauty of trees and plants in their natural forms. He derided clipping and training as 'mathematical'. A year later, Alexander Pope wrote his famous essay 'Verdant Sculpture' describing the practice as 'monstrous'. Garden designers, such as Capability Brown sought to emulate nature in their creation of pastoral parkland settings for stately homes, and for them, topiary had no relevance. Formal gardens were often grubbed out and burnt.

Below: *A striking single topiary in the wonderful garden at Stoneacre.*

But with yet another turn of the wheel of fashion, in this case a return to favor of the Italianate style, the nineteenth century saw a gradual re-introduction of topiary, with a place for both the formal and romantic these later gardens.

When the first settlers came to America and started to establish colonies, their first thoughts of cultivation were to feed themselves and establish crops. But when things became a little easier, and their

Joseph Addison derided clipped and trained yew as 'mathematical'... a year later, Alexander Pope wrote his famous essay 'Verdant Sculpture' describing the practice as 'monstrous'.

aspirations turned to ornamental gardening, topiary was one of the first elements they incorporated. Nathaniel Sylvester is credited with the first introduction of box plants into the gardens of his Long Island manor shortly after it was completed in 1652. Classical examples of boxwood planting can be seen in many faithful garden recreations from this Colonial period, and the American heritage of European-style gardens grew and developed until the present day. The twentieth century saw the establishment of some of the most magnificent topiary gardens in America, indeed the world, including the Ladew Topiary Garden in Maryland, Green Animals in Rhode Island and the Longwood Gardens in Pennsylvania.

As we can see so clearly from the recreation of the Seurat figures at the Old Deaf

School Park in Columbus Ohio, perhaps the greatest American contribution to this garden art has been the introduction of framing. As well as making forms possible that could not be created in any other way, it has also meant that plants that could not necessarily support themselves can be used in topiary. This opens

at Thanksgiving, The Holidays or for a wedding reception - shows how versatile topiary can be, and how stunningly photogenic it is. An entire industry has sprung up all over America and Europe to service this demand, and we can now purchase a simple example, or the materials to create our own unique topiaries

Although topiary is one of the most ancient garden crafts, it continues to be one of the most satisfying and creative, and will surely continue to interest gardeners and homemakers of the future....

up so many creative possibilities, especially for flowers and fragrance. Frames are made from a wide variety of materials, but metal and wire are the most popular.

Despite its fascinating past, the real success of topiary is its huge increase in popularity over the last ten years or so. Perhaps this is because it is such a flexible medium. From a fantastic naturalized display that might have taken decades to perfect, through to a classic lollipop bay in a pot, there really is a topiary opportunity for every garden however large or small.

The current fashion for topiaries to be brought inside for a special occasion – maybe

in many retail outlets. Specialists sell a tremendous variety of plants and accessories, including customized frames. Companies specializing in topiary hire have also sprung up to offer topiary plants in the same way we commission floral arrangements. They often offer valuable pieces that it has taken years to grow, to be picture perfect on the appointed day.

Although topiary is one of the most ancient garden crafts, it continues to be one of the most satisfying and creative, and will surely continue to interest gardeners and homemakers of the future, with its brilliant combination of nostalgia and modernity.

Right: *A double row of cedar tapers, contrasted with a patterned low hedge, gives a formal Mediterranean feel to this garden vista.*

The Ladew Topiary Gardens

Above: *Harvey Ladew rides in hunting pink.*

Dreamy swans float above billowing green waters.... hounds and riders chase a permanently fleeing fox.

Few more colorful figures stride across American cultural history than Harvey Smith Ladew II. He was born into the good time upper middle classes of 1880s New York, so accurately portrayed in the novels of Edith Wharton. Ladew was descended from a wealthy industrial family who were by this time dedicated to spending their money. His uncle, E. Berry Wall rejoiced in the soubriquet 'the King of Dudes'. Freed from the onerous necessity of earning a living by the sale of the Ladew Leather Company, Harvey became a kind of twentieth-century Renaissance man. As he said himself, 'I had money in the bank and no immediate problems.' Although lacking a formal education, Ladew was a clever and articulate man, speaking several languages. He also had the gift of making friends, and was taken up by the glitterati of the time. Thoroughly Anglophile, he spent twenty post-WWI winters foxhunting in England, hobnobbing with the rich, famous and aristocratic. He wrote a book about this part of his life, 'Random Recollections on Fox Hunting', which was published posthumously.

Left (above and below): *The hunt scene at Ladew. One of the most famous topiary creations in the world, it is composed in yew.*

It was his love of the chase that led him to the Maryland hunt country, and to purchase the 250-acre Pleasant Valley Farm in 1929. The original farm gradually evolved into the Ladew Estate as we know it today. He first expanded the original frame-built farmhouse (dating from the eighteenth century) to be an appropriate setting for his extraordinary social life, adding a guest wing, garages and the beautiful Oval Library. Ladew was both exceptionally popular and hospitable, and his guest book was signed by the likes of Lawrence of Arabia, Richard Rodgers, Cole Porter (with whom he played the piano), Noel Coward, Charlie Chaplin, Clark Gable (who rode around the estate with his host), Somerset Maughan, Colette (who reputedly ate snails in bed with Mr. Ladew…) and members of the British royal family.

House finished, Ladew then turned his attention to the gardens, designing 15 garden 'rooms' spanning 22 acres of farmland. These were largely based on the English gardens he loved and remembered from his travels in the 1920s, the work of Gertrude Jekyll being a particular inspiration. In fact, he is considered

Above: *It took nearly fifty years to establish the Ladew gardens.*
They are now in their prime for us to enjoy.

Below: *Harvey Ladew trims one of his famous swans. The wire training frame is still just visible.*

opens theatrically, like a miniature stage set. A selection of lovely artifacts, sculptures and water features offsets the beauty of the planting, including the Ladew pink Tivoli Teahouse, and stunning oval swimming pool.

Today, of course, the gardens are most famous for their fantastic topiary. Dreamy swans float above billowing green waters; seahorses, a unicorn, giraffe, top hat, heart and arrow, butterflies, Chinese junk and Buddha are all sculpted into bizarre topiary forms. Most famous of all, hounds and riders chase a permanently fleeing fox across the lawns. The latter was based on a scene that Ladew had seen in his English foxhunting days, clipped into a Gloucestershire hedge.

Although his inspiration was remarkably diverse, practically, Ladew was completely self-taught. In 1957 he told the Sun magazine 'No one gave me any advice in

to be the first American gardener to follow the tenets of English arts and crafts garden design. The garden was designed with two cross axes to allow for Italianate long vistas, with the garden rooms constructed off each axis. Each room is 'walled in' by manicured hemlock hedges, some of which are now over thirty feet tall. These are trimmed and chiseled into obelisks and garlands, with 'windows' open to the wooded landscape beyond. Each room is devoted to its own particular theme, color or genus, including the White Garden, Victorian Garden, Iris Garden and Berry Garden. Each

gardening, but I have read a lot and knew what I wanted. Now I look back and wonder how I ever got the job done… I think I have managed to create something beautiful and worthwhile in my life' Living until 1976, Ladew himself was a truly extraordinary character, a jet-setter before the phrase was invented. Harvey was most accurately summed up by the tag given to him by English Tatler: 'gardener, sporting art patron and good companion'.

The Ladew Topiary Garden is both the distillation and legacy of his gardening genius, and is now protected in perpetuity by a charitable trust that he himself established.

As he wrote in a 1969 letter to his sister, 'My garden isn't finished yet. I have only worked on it for fifty years and it will take another fifty to finish it.' It has been acclaimed as 'The Best Topiary Garden in America' by the Garden Club of America, and although several other beautiful and notable gardens celebrate this exquisite gardening form, few would dispute the description.

Ladew himself was a great proponent of the Chinese proverb 'If you would be happy all your life, plant a garden.'

Below: *The swans as they are today, floating serenely on the billowing green.*

Old Deaf School Park, Columbus

Fifty-five human forms, three dogs a monkey and a cat are majestically evoked in Mason's dense topiary forms, complete with nineteenth century costumes.

Perhaps the most surreal topiary garden in the world is the extraordinary Old Deaf School Park in Columbus, Ohio. Here, artist and sculptor James T. Mason has created a topiary version of Georges Seurat's 1884-5 painting, 'A Sunday Afternoon on the Island of La Grande Jatte'. The painting is probably the artist's most enduring masterpiece, best known picture, and cultural icon. Seurat's picture is currently owned by the Art Institute of Chicago.

Georges Seurat (1859-1891) is undoubtedly one of the most famous French painters of all time. He was both a member of the Postimpressionist school, and the originator of 'pointillism', a completely original painting technique, where solid forms are constructed by applying tiny, close-packed dots of unmixed color to a white background. This was a direct reaction to the soft and irregular brushstrokes of Impressionism, that often melted colors together. In 'A Sunday Afternoon…' Seurat used this semi-scientific optical style to create a large group of extraordinary volumetric

Left *and* **above:** *Evoking the water scene in the Seurat painting, a topiary steamboat and punt seem to glide on the man-made lake.*

figures, serenely gliding through a perfectly
contoured park. The figures are static and
dignified, most stand gazing into the distance
in formal profile. Adjacent, boaters slide past
on the still and sparkling River Seine.

In the Old Deaf School Park
recreation, fifty-five human
forms, three dogs, a monkey
and a cat are majestically evoked
in Mason's dense topiary forms,
complete with nineteenth
century costumes. A pond has
been constructed to represent
the Seine, and the undulating landscape of the
painting has also been recreated. Fifty two
yew sculptures – boats and figures – appear to
'float' on the pond, evoking the sublime river
life in the painting. The tallest of Mason's
'characters' is over twelve feet tall.

Very much in the tradition of the topiary
form, the recreation of the painting is
somewhat ironic, a living landscape having
been created from the inspiration of a semi-
imaginary landscape several thousand miles

*Right and above: A companionable topiary couple
in the Park, and their originals in the Seurat painting.*

*Previous page: 'A Sunday Afternoon on the Island
of La Grande Jatte' 1884-5 by Georges Seurat. Now
housed at the Art Institute of Chicago.*

and over a hundred years away. The original is about real and imaginary figures in the landscape, whereas the Park is full of fantasy figures in a real and living landscape. As James Mason himself says, 'The topiary garden is both a work of art and a work of nature. It plays on the relationships between nature, art and life.'

One of the most bizarre aspects of the Park is, that being three dimensional, the viewer can wander in amongst Seurat's figures, and view the composition from standpoints the artist himself could never have seen - except in his imagination.

This tremendous project was begun in 1988, when Mason began to make metal frames for each figure in his studio, and

I really love the name of the gift shop at the Park – 'Yewtopia'!

oversaw the planting of nearly a hundred yew trees in the gardens. The sculptured frames form templates for the figures and objects in the topiary 'painting', and guide the degree of bi-annual trimming that each receives from an army of volunteer helpers. The belief that yew

is very slow growing is rather exaggerated, annual growth of at least four inches must be removed to keep the pieces in perfect shape. The frames also offer the plants some protection and support, and keep the integrity of the original composition.

The garden is now internationally recognized, but remains a public space freely open to all. It has been recognized in 'The American Gardener' (the magazine of the American Horticultural Society) as amongst the very best 'secret gardens' in America today, and well worth a visit.

Right *and* **above:** *A group of topiary figures revel in the sunshine, very much as in the original painting.*

Doors of Distinction

The plants combine elegance with a natural softening, while lavender and jasmine introduce an element of fragrance.

Perhaps the most popular of all contemporary uses of topiary is a matching pair of classic shapes used to frame a doorway. If it wasn't so attractive, and almost universally successful, it could be a cliché. It seems that every kind of door, from a simple cottage porch to the imposing portal of a slick urban restaurant can be improved by the addition of a couple of glossy topiaries. Maybe its because the plants combine elegance with a natural softening effect that we find them so appealing.

Now that a much greater variety of plants and shapes are widely available, there's no need to settle for a couple of standard bay balls unless that's your particular fancy. Newly introduced topiary specimens with flowers, berries and fruit ring the changes and broaden the color palette from the traditional dark green. I remember a great pair of standard apple trees outside a grocery store in Sewickley, Pennsylvania. Garden familiars such as lavender and jasmine can introduce an element of welcoming fragrance as topiaries,

Left: A pair of tall lollipops contrasts with pretty foaming blooms to decorate this simple doorway.

Below: *The severe symmetry of this classical portico is reflected by the pair of trim pyramids.*

and even though newcomers like fucshia may not be either evergreen or frost hardy, they can always be replaced by more traditional varieties in the winter season. Framed moss topiaries can also be an expressive way of reflecting seasonal change with the addition of fresh flowers, berries or trinkets. Delicately painted eggs at Easter? Small, bright gourds at Thanksgiving? Personally, I aspire to the fantastic turf and grass-maned lion in 'Walk On the Wild Side'. What could be more imposing than a pair of these heraldic beasts flanking the front door, or more fun?

Further ornament can be added to doorstep topiaries in the form of a wide variety of flowering and foliage plants, either planted with the topiary in its container, or grouped around it, and a wreathe (either seasonal or permanent) can be customized to co-ordinate or contrast with the chosen topiary.

The truly amazing versatility of the door-with-topiary theme is evident through the pages of this book, welcoming guests to christenings, weddings, parties and Christmas celebrations. Here are a few more notable examples of these doors of distinction. Two rather magnificent pyramids in Versailles tubs frame the super-elegant portals of the English Jockey Club, while a pair of open spirals emphasizes the attractive symmetry of these glass doors and windows at the Hintle wedding reception. These sweeping stone steps are rendered slightly less daunting by a whimsical pair of pretty spirals, two more spirals soften this otherwise rather formal entrance.

Below: *Twin spirals contrast with the strong uprights of this porch.*

But for me, the most important aspect of doorstep topiary is, that whatever plant form or decorative alternative you go for, everything must be maintained to a high standard of health and good trim to keep the welcome warm. Absolutely nothing could be sadder and less inviting than the brown and ragged conifer spirals I saw recently outside an Italian restaurant in New York's Little Italy. Definitely not an enticing prospect!

Left *and* **above:** *Naturalized lunettes and containerized spirals define the approach to these two very different doorways.*

Classic Topiary Shapes

Certain classic shapes have endured.

Shapes can also be built up, one upon the other.

Throughout the long and venerable history of topiary, its forms have been derived from many sources of inspiration, ranging from the freakishly extravagant to the restrained and formal. But certain 'classic' shapes have endured, and are as widely used today as ever. These are the essential core of modern topiary and are both widely available commercially, and relatively easy for the amateur enthusiast to achieve, by simple and consistent clipping. The traditional, slow-growing, topiary varieties, such as bay, box and

yew are particularly suitable specimens to create long-lived examples, that retain their outlines with the minimum of maintenance. This also means that container-grown plants don't need frequent re-potting. Of course the other tremendous advantage of many traditionally used plants is that they are evergreen, so that either container-grown or naturalized plants can be used to give year-round interest in all areas of the garden. In the winter, we often move scattered topiaries closer to the house to give us something

Left: *Two simple cones in large terracotta urns decorate and define this otherwise very plain paved area.*

Below: *Two tall standards decorate this fantastic oak lych-gate.*

cheerful to look at! As the pictures of Gatacre Park show, nothing is prettier than a dark, elegant topiary with a crust of sparkling snow, lending a slightly surreal feel to the landscape.

Whilst parterres and knot gardens are inevitably limited to their original sites, freestanding classic shapes can be either naturalized or container grown. Even earth-grown individual plants can be moved a limited number of times. This is how most commercially grown topiaries are established before being potted-on and sold. The legion benefits of containerization have been exploited by generations of topiary gardeners in particular. Possibly the chief amongst these advantages is mobility. The creative designer can re-dress the garden and create variety and interest with the same plants in different locations. In Holland and Germany, for example, standards in containers have been historically used to add height and color contrast to low-growing schemes, where gravel-filled shapes are enclosed by dwarf

Architectural shapes provide a subtle contrast to more freeform planting

hedges. Gardens such as Herren Hausen in Germany use containerized standard orange trees in this way in the months of summer. Standards in pots can also be invaluable to bring height to a young garden where the naturalized plants haven't had a chance to achieve any particular stature. They can also be used to add natural interest, and 'break up' the hard-edged uniformity of the built environment of deck, patio or poolside. The standard bay balls placed around the Roman pool of the Getty Institute in Los Angeles are an extraordinary example of this 'softening' of an intensely formal setting.

Right: *Commercially grown laurel fingers ready for potting up.*

Topiary containers themselves can also make a tremendous contribution to the ornamental potential of the garden, with a fantastic variety of color, texture, style and materials available to the contemporary gardener. From reclaimed garden antiques in stone, lead or cast iron, to terracotta in all its versatile forms, through to minimalist modern containers in cooler materials (such as polished steel, copper or concrete), the variety is virtually infinite. As well as the expressive nature of the 'pots' themselves, their portability can be more than merely decorative. One of the sorrows of this mobile age is that gardeners often plant schemes that they don't have an opportunity to see mature before they move to another property. But containerized topiaries can come with us. We have at least one (now rather huge) home-grown standard bay ball that has moved house

three times in the last thirteen years. Having
known the plant since it started out as three
leaves, we would be devastated to lose it!
It is now doing good service by bringing a
Mediterranean feel to a York stone patio, ably
assisted by several junior colleagues, including
a young olive tree, trained as a standard ball.
Depending on your location, olives can be
slightly tender, but so far so good with this
specimen. We make sure he is kept close to
the house in winter for a little extra warmth
and shelter.

Another advantage of the classic topiary
forms is that, whilst they can add
structure and style to both hard and soft areas
in the garden, they are simple and
unpretentious enough to blend in with other
garden players – trees, shrubs and flowers.
The two large cones in Versailles tubs
demonstrate how a couple of very simple
topiary plants add focus to a soft, informal
planting scheme.

Slightly more elaborate shapes can also
look very dramatic in either interior or exterior
settings, particularly when their formal, dark

Below: *Rows of commercially grown spirals form an abstract composition.*

forms are contrasted with soft, bubbling flowers
in candy colors. These two single standard bays
at Church Farm look delicious with these pretty
blooms cascading from their terracotta
containers. This double ball is an eye-catching
focal point in an otherwise formal setting, whilst
the cypress foliage shows what can be achieved
with a relatively soft-leaved plant. At the other
end of the leaf-size spectrum this naturalized
lonicera nitida is being trained into a tapered
pyramid-shaped iron frame (on page 55). A
more classically shaped pyramid can be seen in
the Levens Hall garden. Pyramids with sloping
sides are also popular.

Left: *Large spirals, one topped with a pom-pom, prettify this black clapboard house.*

Spirals trained from many different plants are extremely en vogue at the moment. They seem to have taken over from balls as the topiary purchase of choice. Here are two good examples, one topped off with a small sphere. They are doing a good job of distracting the eye from a rather large expanse of black clapboard on a New England home, whilst contrasting with the relaxed tendrils of the hanging baskets. Naturalized spirals can both emphasize the structure of the garden, and the many subtle shades of green within it. Spirals may be open (this is where the trunk is visible) or closed (where it is completely concealed by the greenery). Very open spirals can ultimately be trained as corkscrews like that in the group of topiaries in the snow at Gatacre Park. Spirals and corkscrews both require a good deal of skill to establish from scratch, and need to be conscientiously clipped to prevent the shape from degenerating.

The rather abstract photograph of rows of commercially grown spirals (on page 45) shows just how popular this shape is.

More architectural shapes, like the two cypress pillars at the entrance to Stoneacre provide a subtle contrast to more free-form

Left: A homegrown, capped cube in boxwood at Stoneacre.

planting, and in this case to the organic and vernacular nature of the house itself. The Elizabethan-style garden is embellished with several slightly eccentric homegrown topiaries, including the capped cube in box.

Other well-used topiary shapes include 'lunettes' (also know as domes and caps). These are spheres that are grown flush to the ground or their container (like the box balls in the fore-ground of the Twenty-first Century Rock Garden, q.v.).

Shapes can also be built up, one upon the other, as in the Levens Hall garden, where cylinders top cubes, lozenges melt into flattened spheres and cake stands sprout arches. Very long established topiary plants like these often evolve organically as they become simply too big for a single shape. Some of these topiaries have long out-survived their original creators.

Whilst it may not be given to all of us to pass the family plot down through the generations, the rich and on-going tradition of these classic topiary shapes forges a living link for today's gardeners with those of the past.

Above: *A selection of mature show specimens makes an elegant composition.*

Topiary in Winter

Topiaries
don't get
bedraggled in
the snow...

...nor do
they blow
away in the
wind!

Nowhere is the brilliant flexibility of topiary better demonstrated than in its capacity to be both beautiful and useful throughout all seasons, indoors and out.

From emerald cypress fingers shuddering in a sultry haze, or a knot garden filled with dry zone plants, to the stunning effect of large mature shapes sparkling with a halo of snow; strange and startling evergreen forms in a bare landscape. No other garden element is so compelling, whatever the weather.

For me, no other form of gardening works so consistently and effectively in our homes and gardens, through all the months of the year.

It is not only the evergreen nature of many topiary plants that gives them value in the winter garden, but their combination of elegance and playfulness that gladdens the eye and lifts the drabbest scene. Topiaries don't get bedraggled in the snow or driving rain, and don't blow away in the wind! The portability of containerised plants also gives us the opportunity to use slightly more tender

Left: *This very curious creature at Gatacre Park looks like an interstellar visitor. The snow adds to the strange beauty of the scene.*

varieties outside on not-so-cold days, so that
some of our hardier summer favorites can
show their faces for at least some of the
colder months.

How effective this simple spiral looks with
glistening snow highlighting its sinuous curves.

**From emerald cypress
fingers shuddering in a
sultry haze... to the stunning
effect of large mature shapes
sparkling with a halo of
snow; strange and startling
evergreen forms in a
bare landscape.**

Naturalized plants can also come into
their own at this time of year, there is so
much less in the garden to distract our attention
from them. Plants that have been grown
principally for structure, and to contrast with
flower-bearing species, suddenly become stars in
their own right. As well as introducing color with
their foliage, with variegated species making a
tonal impact, topiary plants can also bear berries
in many different colors, pastel or fiery.

Left: *This surreal group of topiaries at Gatacre
Park glistens under a crust of pristine snow.*

The breathtaking scene at Gatacre Park shows to great effect the surreal loveliness of these eccentric creations crusted with snow. The complex topiaries look even more chiseled in the hard winter light, and the topiaries can also look wonderful grouped with pillar candles flickering atmospherically.

Moss-filled topiary can be a fantastic winter resource, to grace the home inside and out. What could be more romantic than a delightful

The poignant contrast between summer and winter topiary is exemplified by sculptures in the Deaf School Park – in June, relaxed and playful, but in December the snow-dusted characters seem to huddle together for comfort.

bizarre shapes cast long moody shadows in the low sun. What could possibly be more magical than snow on the Ladew Topiary Garden swans?

The decorative potential of container grown topiaries can be particularly useful in the winter, to replace unavailable or expensive flowers. I recall standard laurels flanking the gothic porch at Battisford Church, simply decorated with ribbons for a winter christening.

Topiaries can also be used to great effect inside the home at this time of year. Grouped with other seasonal plants, such as poinsettias, or garlanded with traditional foliage - holly, ivy or mistletoe. Velvety

centerpiece decorated with hothouse roses and lilies, whilst making the most of an expensive winter luxury?

For me, the most poignant contrast between summer and winter topiary is exemplified by the living Seurat sculptures in the Old Deaf School Park, Columbus, Ohio. In the verdant green of the Park in June, the figures look relaxed and playful, soaking up the sun-shine, dabbling on the river. In December, the snow-dusted characters seem isolated in the bleak landscape, huddling together for comfort.

Topiary plants can also bear berries in many different colors, pastel or fiery.

Left: *A topiary couple, at the Old Deaf School Park in Columbus, huddle together tenderly in the snow.*

Summer Topiary

Clipping,
pleaching,
pollarding
and espalier
training...

...may all
be employed
to achieve
the finished
results.

Topiary can play many roles in the summer garden. It can be used as part of the garden structure, a transitional element to dovetail indoor and outdoor spaces, or a wonderfully restrained counterpoint to the voluptuous and heady growth of the season.

Indeed, the uses of topiary in the summer garden are a mass of contradiction. Topiaries can be used to define and frame a view, or showcase a special garden feature, whilst simultaneously concealing an unattractive vista. Or it may simply screen a more private area of the garden, such as the poolside or a vegetable patch. Topiary can be used to link a garden to the wider landscape, or compartmentalize a private garden room. It can define an architectural feature, or be used to construct such an element. It is such an unbelievably flexible medium that it can be used as a sound barrier, and carrier of perfume at the same time.

Several techniques may be used together or singly to achieve these effects with topiary on a grand scale. Clipping, pleaching, pollarding and espalier training may all be employed to

Left: *This clipped boxwood and stone seat is an organic part of the garden, resting against the ivy-clad wall.*

achieve the finished results. Clipping means exactly what it says. Pleaching is where trees with flexible branches are woven together to form a vertical screen, or perhaps a 'roof' to a garden corridor. Pollarding is the cutting back of living tree canopies into ornamental shapes. Espalier training is where trees and shrubs (often fruit trees) are pruned into an open fan shape, often with the support of a wall.

A wonderfully restrained counterpoint to the heady growth of the season

What could be more spectacular than the architectural topiaries of Levens Hall, contrasting so brilliantly with banks and beds of vivid and luxuriant summer flowers? Somehow, the massive and apparently ageless structures, emphasize the delicate and ephemeral nature of the summer blooms.

At the Ladew Gardens, the topiary-decked terrace of telescopic forms around Pleasant Valley House echoes its simple architectural lines and angles, whilst drawing the visitor deeper into the garden.

Right: *These telescopic topiaries around Harvey Ladew's Pleasant Valley House beckon the visitor into the garden.*

The topiary sculptures and structures in the garden's many different rooms are used either to offset the vibrant color themes (pink, yellow, white, red and gold) or to act as a theatrical backdrop to naturalistic planting of swathes of softly drifting flowers and foliage.

In a different take on the 'architectural' potential of topiary, this wonderful garden seat uses a stone slab and box arms to construct a feature that is both practical, and constitutes an organic part of the garden. The seat back rests on a completely ivy-clad wall so that the

Below: *This precise and geometric garden room is designed around the extraordinary sundial timepiece.*

stone urn and seat seem to float unsupported. More traditionally, the huge topiaries flanking these stone steps at Hazlebury Manor blend the 'built' garden into the rolling lawn, whilst seemingly helping to support the roof structure of the romantically crumbling pavilion.

In a complete contrast of mood, nothing could be more precise and geometric than this enclosed and slightly mysterious garden compartment, designed around the beautiful sundial. In this slightly Dali-esque setting, time seems to stand still in this fragment of ordered universe. There is just a glimpse of the outside world through the arched doorway, but the topiary filled rooms seem to go on forever. This kind of design could work in any season, but in the summer, the banquettes of box, and balls and cubes of yew, make this surreal garden a shadow box for the interplay of light and shade.

These massive cedar arches transect this garden into a series of slices, each with a different feel and theme. The huge structures both echo each other, and frame a series of internal garden views.

In the smaller, less conceptual garden, topiary is particularly valuable in melting the hardscaped outdoor spaces – decks, patios and poolside – into the green garden. Instant containerized topiaries are particularly useful, and can also introduce color and perfume into an otherwise barren area. The slightly sharp edges of this new stone path leading to this simple wooden gazebo are somewhat softened by the addition of two cypress pom-poms in pretty terracotta pots. These aren't quite so precise as box or yew, and give off a pleasant

Right and above: These two very different settings show how both naturalized and container-grown topiaries can complement the summer garden.

woody aroma. In this setting, they also offer an ever-so-slightly formal contrast to the countryside beyond the garden. This 'greening' effect is taken to its logical conclusion on this urban balcony, where the trained spiral and planted pots reflect the mature trees in the square garden below.

Huge topiaries blend the 'built' garden into the rolling lawn.

Topiary hedges and boxes can also be used to frame and highlight a particular garden feature. In a slightly surreal touch, this octagonal box 'planter' emphasizes the height and open structure of the exotic potted palm, whilst the network of clipped hedges contrasts with the white colonial-style house and the simple 'drift' planting of Hidcote lavender, daisies and Sweet William. This structural design has the advantage that, if the palm needs to be over-wintered under cover, the basic garden design remains intact.

Below: *This octagonal boxwood planter may have taken at least ten years to reach this immaculate state. It contrasts brilliantly with the waving palm fronds.*

On a more cozy and domestic scale, topiary can be used as a positive kind of screen to define an area of the garden for our own private enjoyment. This yellow clapboard garden shed is made both homey and magical by the addition of a perfect, miniaturized topiary garden and festoons of pink wallflowers. Completely informal, it contrives to be ultimately pretty as it nestles in the garden hinterland. What could be more fun than a secret escape to this tiny garden 'house', a secluded retreat from the garden, just for us?

Right: *This yellow clapboard shed provides a lovely private retreat from the public garden.*

A Walk on the Wild Side

Topiary can also do fantasy and humor

So versatile a medium is topiary that as well as elegance, grandeur, and the surreal, it can also do fantasy and humor. The bucolic foxhunt at Ladew, the jolly teddies and ubsurd animals at Gatacre Park, or the full-sized Mickey and friends welcoming guests to Disneyland California, all raise a smile.

Framing originated in the US but is now popular everywhere, especially in Europe. This has been a real benefit to the creative topiarist, as it means that the plants do not need to be entirely self-supporting. As well as enabling the professional to create fantastically large and complicated shapes (I have seen full-scale steam trains and horse-drawn carriages) it also enables the amateur enthusiast to develop precise shapes and compositions on a domestic scale.

This crouching lion is created from a frame filled with mossy turf and long grasses. 'YES' is filled with box, but yew, lonicera nitida or many other equally suitable plants could have been used (q.v. the plant glossary). All that is required to frame-train living plants is a sharp pair of hand pruning shears and some conscientious trimming. For most varieties, this should start in the spring, and be done every other month throughout the summer.

Left: This fantastic topiary sculpture of Mr. Fearon's face is a living tribute to the gardener.

Clipping should cease at the first hint of frost, as this can damage new shoots, and ultimately kill the plant. Although amazingly flexible, framing is particularly useful for small projects (where precision is highly desirable) and so it is ideal for private gardens. There is a ready-made frame available for virtually any shape you can think of – chickens, dragons, fairies - or the creative can construct their own design.

The freeform sculpture of Mr. Fearon's face, on the other hand, is rather more personal and quirky. It is a complete original. The reposeful subject seems to be snoozing in the warm evening sun, the golden lonicera nitida glowing attractively. What a brilliant idea, to commemorate the gardener himself in the living green.

Above left and right: *This fantastic lion couchant was created using this wire frame, covered in velvety turf and long ornamental grass.*

Wedding Topiary

America's greatest contribution to topiary is the wire frame

The growing popularity of topiary is very much reflected in its increasingly regular appearances at wedding celebrations. The dark solid elegance of the topiary plants contrasts so well with the floaty whites and pastels of traditional wedding decorations. The plants themselves are very photogenic, and a perfectly matched pair of classic spheres or spirals makes a lovely composition to welcome guests at the church doors, both softening and echoing the architectural forms. Here two lollipops inject a

Left: *This fantastic Gothic arch is softened by these two simple standard lollipops, to welcome the wedding guests.*

delightful element of fun to the massive gothic doorway to this church, and offer a subtle contrast of living green to the dominant stone. Equally, an outdoor wedding could be stunningly decorated with some lovely romantic emblems, maybe of serenely gliding swans, fanciful cherubs or pastoral animals grazing peacefully. In a garden setting, the existing plants and flowers can offer a wonderful counterpoint to formal or whimsical topiaries. The humor of reverse scale in particular - huge teacups and saucers or tiny dinosaurs – is a

delicate, trailing floral arrangements, and act as a formal and restrained counterpoint to prevent flowing gauze, tulle and ribbon from being overpoweringly bland and sweet. Another option could be tabletop topiaries - either low pruned plants, or moss-filled wire shapes, as part of the overall design. These could be ornamented with ribbons, wedding favors or fresh flower heads in the theme colors of the wedding. The topiaries themselves could be sculpted in forms significant to the couple, or universally romantic symbols such as hearts,

Nothing is more evocative than perfume, and an aroma of clipped lavender, rosemary or honeysuckle brings a sensual dimension to the decor.

great element of the craft of topiary that can be fully explored in a landscape tableau. Indeed, some of the most famous topiary gardens in the world, such as Ladew in Maryland or Leeds Castle in Kent, can be hired for upscale wedding celebrations.

At the reception, standard plants in containers can provide an elegant contrast to

entwined rings or doves. Topiary is such a flexible design medium that the possibilities are virtually endless. A one-off occasion such as a wedding could be an ideal opportunity to hire large mature plants or to commission a stunning wire-framed masterpiece. Plant designers can work closely with the couple or wedding organizer and explain the ornamental

possibilities of topiary. Many suppliers now cater for this trend.

The plant containers can also be an element in the overall design, either decorated with wedding draperies, or revealed to make their own statement. Maybe these could be supremely classical lead planters, decorated with garlands or cherubim, or unusual containers reflecting the interests of the wedding couple.

It has been said that America's greatest contribution to the art form of topiary is the wire frame, as it opens up so many design possibilities not previously available. Many more plants can be used if supported by a frame, and more intricate designs become possible. This is particularly useful in the context of a wedding where every celebration aims to be unique. Frames can be used in- or outdoors, and can be filled with either living plants or moss and florists' materials. Ivy in particular has become immensely popular for its effectiveness and ease of use. Using a frame also means that a variety of species can be planted together and trained into a shape.

Whereas European topiarists almost invariably use evergreens, American practicioners of the craft often employ a much wider spectrum of plants, including flowering varieties. These can be color coordinated to stunning effect.

The other element that should not be overlooked as an aspect of wedding topiary is scent. Nothing is more evocative than perfume, and a delicious aroma of clipped or trained lavender, rosemary or honeysuckle could bring a new and sensual dimension to the decor. Depending on the time of year, or the desired effect, perfumes could range from the fresh and subtle (maybe juniper or lemon eucalyptus) to the outrageously heady and voluptuous (jasmine,

scented geranium?). The hotter the day, the more fully the plant scents will develop, so care should be taken that the bouquet of the wine or the flavors of the wedding banquet are not overpowered. But what a wonderful way to deeply imprint memories of the day, and to provide a quick way of recalling it to mind with just a quick sniff of the appropriate plant.

Right: *The entrance to this fantastic wedding marquee is signposted by this pair of lovely open spirals.*

possibilities of topiary. Many suppliers now cater for this trend.

The plant containers can also be an element in the overall design, either decorated with wedding draperies, or revealed to make their own statement. Maybe these could be supremely classical lead planters, decorated with garlands or cherubim, or unusual containers reflecting the interests of the wedding couple.

It has been said that America's greatest contribution to the art form of topiary is the wire frame, as it opens up so many design possibilities not previously available. Many more plants can be used if supported by a frame, and more intricate designs become possible. This is particularly useful in the context of a wedding where every celebration aims to be unique. Frames can be used in- or outdoors, and can be filled with either living plants or moss and florists' materials. Ivy in particular has become immensely popular for its effectiveness and ease of use. Using a frame also means that a variety of species can be planted together and trained into a shape.

Whereas European topiarists almost invariably use evergreens, American practicioners of the craft often employ a much wider spectrum of plants, including flowering varieties. These can be color coordinated to stunning effect.

The other element that should not be overlooked as an aspect of wedding topiary is scent. Nothing is more evocative than perfume, and a delicious aroma of clipped or trained lavender, rosemary or honeysuckle could bring a new and sensual dimension to the decor. Depending on the time of year, or the desired effect, perfumes could range from the fresh and subtle (maybe juniper or lemon eucalyptus) to the outrageously heady and voluptuous (jasmine,

scented geranium?). The hotter the day, the more fully the plant scents will develop, so care should be taken that the bouquet of the wine or the flavors of the wedding banquet are not overpowered. But what a wonderful way to deeply imprint memories of the day, and to provide a quick way of recalling it to mind with just a quick sniff of the appropriate plant.

21st Century Topiary

Topiary is becoming almost universal

Perhaps the real test of any art form is its longevity. Only the best survive. If this is the litmus test, topiary is a roaring success by any standards.

The undoubted key to the on-going popularity of topiary is its flexibility and usefulness. It is a garden resource throughout the seasons. Topiaries can be used indoors and out. The form it takes may be formal, luxuriant, high art or entirely kitsch. Topiary works in any number of different scales from tiny birds in pots to massive structures that have been grown over centuries. The shapes may be simple, composite, fantastically complicated. The plant material used in the topiaries of today is massively diverse, new species are being added all the time. Topiary is becoming almost universal, but seems to have avoided becoming the kind of dreary cliché of so many 'fashion' statements. Personally, I think that this is something to do both with the vibrant creativity that so many gardeners have lavished on the medium, and the fact that the plants themselves are living, constantly changing and regenerating.

Topiaries also work in any number of different settings, from the crumbling classical garden of an ancient mansion to the sharp modern lines exemplified so brilliantly

Above: *This row of photographs in a Brompton Road gallery is interspersed with identical miniature standards.*

by this exhibition garden from the Chelsea Flower Show, 'Twenty-first century Topiary'.

The clean, white space of this outdoor garden room is softened with the addition of naturalized lunettes in box, containerised cedar pom-poms and pot-grown wall plants. Although the concept behind the garden is completely 'now', and the hardscape uncompromising, the elements are essentially traditional - pool, path, flowerbeds. Even the fire bowl could be considered as a modern take on a bonfire.

By contrast, the indoor use of these simple topiary shapes in a Brompton Road art gallery highlights the simple elegance that topiary can bring to almost any setting. The row of single lollipops complements a row of framed photographs and an arrangement of double pom-poms and spirals offsets the clinical white of the gallery walls.

This indoor use of both living topiary and filled frames at parties, weddings and in retail and business space, is perhaps the most definable contribution of the modern enthusiast to this venerable tradition. What will come next? Who knows...

Above: *This is a truly twenty-first century topiary garden, with lunettes and pom-poms decorating the bland white space.*

Traditional Topiary Tools

Handheld tools seem natural to this fine-tuning of nature

The tools needed for topiary are simple and remain little changed from the introduction of the craft. The Romans began by using sharp knives for precise trimming, but the early seventeenth century saw the introduction of wooden handled shears with the 'scissor' action we use to this day. Hand held pruning shears with a double blade were a later introduction, and knives were used up until the nineteenth century. Billhooks were invaluable for pollarding and pleaching, and a scythe might be used for more dramatic 'lopping'. These tools would have been originally forged by hand from Hardened steel. The materials may have evolved slightly, to stainless steel perhaps, but their basic shape and function remains constant.

There is something pleasantly warm and reassuring about the low-tech nature of the equipment required to practice the craft. Handheld tools seem natural to this fine-tuning of nature, it is always better to take off a little growth at a time. This is both for the sake of the plant, and to avoid a drastic mistake that could ruin years of training. Gas-powered or electric hedge clippers can be used on big, regular topiary structures (or hedges of course), but some species just don't take well to power tools (such as holly or bay) because, once cut, the leaves may discolour and die.

The skill, creativity and patience of the gardener are still the prerequisites for successful topiary. Most topiarists really enjoy the pottering nature of a little light pruning, as we can see from the photograph of Harvey Ladew trimming his swans, in a very mellow and contemplative way.

Left: *Simple tools – a billhook, shears, hand held pruning clippers and a scythe rest against the tool-shed door.*

Topiary Plant Directory

Bay

Laurus Nobilis is one of the most recognisable and popular of the topiary plants. Bay is a sun loving and yet climate tolerant plant. Its leaves have been used in cookery since early times. Bay leaves were also used to make laurel wreathes for victors in the classical world, hence 'laureate'.

Standard bay lollipops are typically used to frame doorways, and the trunks can be gently twisted to form spirals for an exotic touch. They are slow growing but have lovely, dense, fragrant growth. Its best to trim the bushes by hand to avoid ugly and damaging cuts to the leaves. This needs to be done twice annually to maintain a good shape, once in early summer, and again in late summer.

Boxwood

Buxus is the king of small to medium scale topiary, parterre and bed edging, and is the first choice for many projects. The plant has been in use for thousands of years, and is incredibly versatile for any number of ornamental uses. The small glossy green leaves are attractive, and respond well to trimming, having a moderate rate of growth. As the name suggests, the standard variety, *buxus sempervirens* is the most hardy, but there are many different forms, including colored and variegated (*buxus elegantissima* has leaves edged in whitish cream, whilst *buxus notata* has yellow-tipped leaves) and dwarf (*buxus sempervirens suffruticosa* will happily form a hedge as low as 6 inches). Where a larger project is envisaged, the slightly taller growing *buxus handsworthiensis* is recommended. Generally, box flowers are insignificant, so it really the form of the plants that give interest. Box is not demanding, thriving on a range of well-drained soils, but appreciates feeding - liquid seaweed is ideal. Clipping should be done twice over the summer, but no pruning should be attempted when there is a chance of frost, as the cold can get in through the exposed ends and kill the plant. The very unpleasant Box Blight is one of the few problems suffered by these tolerant, hard-working plants, and as yet there is no cure. Grubbing out and burning any affected bushes is the only control.

Holly

Ilex is one of the most recognisable plants used for topiary and has everything going for it – fabulous glossy evergreen foliage, pretty (generally white) flowers, fabulous berries (mostly red, sometimes yellow, or even black) – except for the spikes! The only other potential problem with this plant is its slow growth, slower even than yew. In fact, there are several hundred species of this versatile beauty, some are variegated, golden or silvery. Most varieties are fully hardy. The plants can make superb, if slow growing, hedges and lovely simple topiaries adorned with their own flowers and berries. Hand clipping is required to preserve the leaves.

Lonicera

Lonicera Nitida is actually a member of the honeysuckle family. A fast growing shrub, it can grow to up to four feet in height (1.8m) and can be used for hedging or topiary shapes. The new growth is so soft that it can be snipped with a pair of scissors. The plants are reputedly fully hardy, but a very severe winter can be fatal. Twice yearly clipping is required to keep a shape.

Olive

There are around 10-15 varieties of *olea europaea* available to the gardener, and their greyish green foliage is very evocative of the Mediterranean. However, they can be quite tender so care must be taken. The fruits tend not to ripen outside a fairly narrow climactic zone. Simple standards can be created with gentle trimming.

Yew

Taxus is the king of large, long-living topiary plants, a small genus of evergreen conifers. It is incredibly flexible, and can be trained into any number of simple and complex shapes. Its growth rate is fairly slow, so a seven-foot high hedge could take up to a decade to mature. The plants should be clipped little and often through the growing season to establish a firm outline that will retain sharp outlines and details. Shapes can be made up from a single plant, or several trees planted together, which gives a great flexibility for scale. Virtually all parts of the plant are poisonous, so care needs to be taken as to where the trees are sited. Yew is fully hardy, and tolerant of a wide range of growing conditions and soil types, but its needs to be in a well drained position. This is one topiary plant that does not object to the use of electric hedge-trimmers.